A Coyote in The Garden

A Coyote
in the Garden
by An Painter

edited, with a foreword by N. Scott Momaday

Confluence Press   **Lewiston, Idaho**

ISBN 0-917-652-69-X
Library of Congress Card Number 87-72518

Publication of this book is made possible by grants from the Idaho
Commission on the Arts, a State agency, and the National Endowment
for the Arts in Washington, D.C., a Federal agency.

Published by:

Confluence Press, Inc.
Lewis Clark State College
8th Avenue & 6th Street
Lewiston, Idaho 83501

Distributed to the trade by:

Kampmann & Company
9 East 40th Street
New York, New York 10016

Foreword

An Painter is an intelligent and sensitive woman, and she is an artist of real distinction. When I first met her—on an airplane, as I remember, flying from Washington, D.C. to Dallas, Texas—she told me that she was a photographer. Indeed she is. Her photographs, several of which I now own, are exceptional. She has the sure, quick eye of a master photojournalist, an Eisenstaedt, say, the patience and the spontaneity. She has the gift of composing a photograph immediately in terms of symmetry, proportion, and design. Her photographs are strong, lyrical, and telling. Most of all, they are imaginative. Like other artists—writers and painters and musicians—she is able to express her spirit definitively in her work.

It was with a certain experience of wonder that I discovered she was a poet, too. I need not, I think, comment particularly upon her poems, for they are here, and they speak most eloquently for themselves. Her chosen form to date is the Japanese haiku, and she does the form absolute justice, I believe. She does not hesitate to depart on occasion from the fixed definition of haiku—there are not always seventeen syllables; the poems do not always bear specifically upon the seasons. But the incisive spirit of the form is realized remarkably. The economy, the precision of her verse, the profound clarity of image, these are beyond question. In her conciseness and concentration she reminds us of Emily Dickinson, perhaps. There is the same shorthand, as it were, the same uncanny turn of phrase, the same perception of wilderness.

An Painter's poems are transcendental in the root sense of that word. In a way, I would like to state that they center upon the great natural world of the American Southwest, for that is a landscape she knows very well, and it is the principal habitat of coyote, the central figure in this collection. But the truth of the matter is, her poems cannot be consigned to a particular geography, a particular time, or even a particular way of looking at the world. They are universal.

I find myself coming back to these poems again and again. They are like prisms in that their brilliance shifts from surface to surface in the changing light. They are vibrant; they are preeminently alive.

Long live Coyote! And from An Painter, let there be many more poems to come.

N. Scott Momaday

Black punctuated with
blue, the methodic stars
on a moonless night

1965

The red leaf swirling
in a crystalline pool now
glimmers in my hand.

1967

1

Sparrow in the dawn
dimly remembers summer:
song of rippling sun.

1967

Sea gull cry overheard,
and the thoughts fly guilty to
the present once more.

1967

Summer run, now your
bright orange face hides behind
blue-grey streaks of rain.

1976

Squirrel lies cat-like,
belly flat against the pavement,
panting in summer.

1976

3

After death there is
No life; nor is there life, nor
Death. There simply is.

1977

At the garden's edge
the late red rose grows next to
wild purple asters.

1977

I have seen rainbows
arcing twice about the sun...
Will that be enough?

1977

Fallen persimmons
gathered with violets...
The sun sets in my hands.

1977

Days after the storm
the north-facing pine branches
still glisten with ice.

1977

From horseback I see
the atamasco lillies...
we pass quietly.

1977

6

Summer cornflowers
grow so tall— Is that a
rabbit hidden underneath?

1977

My landlord's unkind,
so he won't know his chestnut
tree bore fruit this year.

1977

The moon took my breath
away, suddenly rising
so large and orange.

1977

Stiff feathers puffed out
Into the morning sun...
Red-tailed hawk awakens.

1977

If I close my eyes,
tight, the icy branches are
covered with blossoms.

1978

Today the buds on
my dogwood tree first held the
promise of blooming.

1978

When woods quicken from
brown to red, brittle branches
show supple promise.

1978

The hot, sweet breath of
honeysuckles surrounds my
body with summer.

1978

10

The hawk sleeps upright
Except for his head which is
bent over, like this

1978

It's summer and my
hawks have all gone. Now their trees
are dull to look at.

1978

11

The leaf in my hand
fell from a tropical tree:
red, orange, green— dead.

1978

I dreamed I was with
persimmons on their tree (our
tree)—small, round, orange.

1978

12

Blueberry Island
circled by deep cold waters:
gentian blooms unseen.

1978

Fragrance-drunk moths fly
uncertainly among
fallen persimmons.

1980

Red-tailed hawk comes to
look for me. Have I wandered
too far? Am I lost?

1980

The foals lie flat
in the spring grass,
with just their little bellies showing.

1984

14

Unmistakeable
turkey vulture soars gently
on the first Spring wind.

1984

This spring the crow flies
in circles; is he snapping
insects? or playing?

1980

15

Our words between us:
Visible mist suspended
on night's wilderness.

1980

Four paws in the air,
ears flattened against the hearth:
Cat with Cedar Smoke

1985

16

Night falls. Then a slow
rock thumps; it is the Artist's
tortoise, pale and white.

1986

Nourishing myself
with my own flesh, all that's left
a gaping jawbone.

1986

17

On this
morning a large white
cloud from its berth in the canyon
set sail.

1985

Everything, I will
let go of it all. Except
my passion I keep.

1986

18

A Paraphrase

For John

The full moon is held
within a pail of water.
Splash! It is daylight!

1986

Meditating. Unformed
cloud bowl holds
its apparition—a comet.

1986

19

Unsubtle tulips,
with yawning mouths much too red,
Go to sleep! It's night.

1986

Mountain opalescent,
its memory a ring
unto my finger.

1986

Thick black lava fields
wear a headdress of green reeds
that shake with the wind.

1986

For Bobbi

Glaciers melt and
crystalline rigidity
becomes flowing water.

1986

21

Four
Warrior Poems

Just for his mirror
the fierce gaze of the warrior
with the tender heart.

1986

Warrior sitting
perfectly still: only
his heart is breathing.

1986

Chant this mantra for
/cockroach, crocodile and crab/
the end of the world.

1986

It is my regard
on you, waking you, that is
a warrior's kiss.

1986

23

Infrequent sunrise
appears at the insistence
of my alarm-cat.

1986

Barn swallows and stop
lights delineate the in-
visible insects

1986

Dusk: grey cat carries
cantaloupe rind away from
advancing turkey.

1986

In early June the
grasshoppers finish eating
my chrysanthemums.

1986

25

Below the mountain,
clouds, awaiting a warm breeze
to untether them.

1986

On still-blue summer
mornings, the buoy boat puts
our river to sleep.

1986

26

Rowing hard downriver
during rain—water dripping
within, without.

1987

Quiet. Just listen—
channels of liquid fire course
within us. Hear it?

1986

Hold your ears, your eyes
tight shut. Pretend you cannot
hear the Earth's heart beat.

1986

Coyote Love

Coyote leaping
grabs my heart between his teeth
and breaks it, for fun.

1986

When the coyote
Howls at the moon he creates
Love from sagebrush dust.

1986

29

Coyote picks his
sharp teeth with the slender bones
of his beloved.

1986

The wind is a harp
to howl upon—coyote
plays for his lover.

1986

The night tamarisk?
Shadowed cholla? Rabbitbrush?
Coyote in love.

1986

Coyote dreams and
salt cedar, stars, love, moths and
moonlight live and die.

1986

31

The tuft of grama
grass tickles coyote's nose
He sniffs it again.

1986

Laughter and tears curled
beneath indigo branches:
Coyote asleep.

1986

Coyote tells me
that I am beautiful.
I think he's lying.

1986

Coyote in love
eating prickly pear flowers,
admiring rabbits.

1986

Desert lightning strikes
and kills the cactus
but coyote learns to fly.

1986

Subliming dew on
his silver coat, coyote
distills white moondrops.

1986

34

Wind and coyote
race through the desert looking out
for tumbleweeds.

1986

For Louis Sahagun

Within saguaro
cactus eyes watch a feather-
loving coyote

1986

Coyote lover
dines upon marrow sucked from
his beloved's bones.

1986

Desert winds change and
coyote discovers dust-
devils. So he howls.

1986

Full moon in Autumn
coyote and tumbleweed
twirl across the sands.

1986

Ardent coyote
whispers hypnotic words while
nibbling my earlobe.

1986

37

Contemplating stars
one by one, coyote dreams
a desert to life.

1986

For Faeylyn

Desert prayer flag:
coyote milagro hangs
on a cactus thorn.

1986

Underwater

Inbreath, outbreath, there!
Spanish grunts together...
oh-oh, barracuda...

1986

Small, sleek, and silver
barracuda, hiding be
              hind a mangrove root.

1986

By himself, the small
top-piece waving about; a
mexican hat. Fish?

1986

Big eyes, many spines
under the coral ledge
cardinal fish hover.

1986

Holding my warm hands
very still, a tiny green
pufferfish within.

1986

Eyes closed, haloes of
sunlight flash from bay side to
side, slow afternoon.

1986

41

If I clasp this piece
of shell I hold a million
years of life and more.

1986

Sand fleas hop stinking
seaweed piles and men-of-war
floats then sting my knees.

1986

Sand and shells sucked out
whooshing in, tinkling again—so
shells tumble about.

1986

A beach whose sandy
winds blow sideways, one
rare marbled murrelet.

1986

Drinking too much rum
the Caribbean can be
too cold for swimming.

1986

Diving this crevasse
to see a moray eel,
my nipples tighten.

1986

44

Once there were squid, pink,
everywhere, blue, their eyes
gleaming, green pink red.

1986

Ripples pass under
neath the waves. It is the sand
travelling to Spain.

1986

Click, click, click, snapping
shrimp click click their tiny claws,
click, click, much too small.

1986

Down, blue chromis gleam
among broken coral heads
down, leading me on.

1986

Mindlessly manta
rays somersault in the air
vaulting reality.

1986

Whales at Fortuna
heard underwater, unseen:
warm-hearted voices.

1986

Horseshoe crab, with his
eyes not separate from his
shell: primitive.

1986

Glaciers float past
warm lagoons: whales returning
for frangipani.

1986

48

Endless toothy jaws—
a barracuda, curious,
swims visiting by.

1986

Yes, that is a shark.
Maybe I can wave my limbs
slowly, sea-fannish.

1986

Antennae long and
quivering: dinner within
a niche? Too pretty.

1986

Coral, sponge, and seaweed,
a little shell, perhaps two—
spider crab festooned.

1986

50

A hawksbill turtle
surfaces, sees me and I him:
explosive swimming.

1986

Diadema, spiny
painful beauty whose journeys
are solitary.

1986

Snatching kelp fronds from
beneath the sea, humpback whale
flies south with streamers.

1986

One tufted puffin
paddles close, camouflaged by
solitariness.

1986

Arcing from behind
molten blue glaciers, toothed whales
pursuing puffins.

1986

Crunching coral heads,
showering the reef with sand:
stoplight parrotfish.

1986

Sunlight waving on
turtle grass undulating
hiding sea urchins.

1986

Mangrove root shoots up
into the air then plunges
through salty water.

1986

54

Ah, I have swallowed
water and I am dying...
Not here, with beauty!

1986

The Wilderness Poems

Thin-breathed steps leading
one in front of the last one—
stillness, snow, then elk.

1986

Once, when we went up
the mountain in silence, we
heard the mountain speak.

1986

Unseen except in wilderness, parry primrose
blooming in shadows.

1986

Hawk flies the scree slope,
gyring higher, then passing
over my eyesight.

1986

Boots into icy
water up to the ankles—
I *will* cross this stream.

1986

I have taught him this,
too: in wilderness trout will
swim into your hands.

1986

58

Book in the pocket:
camp to be made before sun-
set stops city time.

1986

Midnight cows bumping
into my tent—dinosaurs
brought thrashing to life.

1986

Calypso orchid,
hellebore and tanager, trails
by name, not number.

1986

Swift mists above pines
sudden snow and windy blasts
of colder danger.

1986

Boil dammit. Numb mind,
cold fingers stuck together.
Dammit coffee, boil!

1986

Ah hah, first sight from
the sleeping bag—a pika,
eating my bootlace!

1986

I made a cup with
a hellebore leaf; the water
became sacrament.

1986

Concealed by cowslip,
thirteen-striped ground squirrel is
smaller than his name.

1986

Tuft of whitish fur
snagged along the trail, deer hooves,
snowy November.

1986

From stars to cygnets
an unbroken wilderness
mindful of lineage.

1986

63

Sphingid moth visits
queen anne's lace; it topples, so
he visits iris.

1986

Map-intermittent,
this torrent separates me
from a moss-soft bed.

1986

July wilderness:
an unexpected snowbank
compells attention.

1986

Five days of hiking
I *must* wash my hair—
expecting photographers?

1986

65

A bed of sharp and
difficult stones, the summit,
uneasy sleeping.

1986

The clouds. One's self then
becomes a wilderness, clouds
being within us.

1986

Biographical Note

An Painter lives in a small village outside Albu-
querque, New Mexico. She was born and raised in West-
chester County, New York, and graduated from McGill
University in Montreal, where she studied French and
Italian. She has lived and traveled extensively outside
the United States, including Europe and the U.S. Vir-
gin Islands. She has been employed as a biological tech-
nician, a florist, and a graphic artist. In New Mexico,
where she has spent the last nine years, she makes her
living from photography and mediation.